ADVENTURE S

SWIMMING *and* SUB-AQUA

Michael Jay

Kingfisher Books

Designed and produced by:
David Jefferis

Edited by:
Jackie Gaff

Illustrated by:
Robert and Rhoda Burns
James Robins
Michael Roffe

Photographs supplied by:
Philip Anderson
Tony Duffy/All Sport
M Edge
David Jefferis
Eileen Langsley/Supersport
Photographs
H Lindner/ZEFA
Raibeart MacDougall
Voightmann/ZEFA
Warren Williams/ZEFA

With special thanks to Nigel
Dobinson of the St Albans
Sub Aqua Club for his help
and guidance, and to
Lillywhites Ltd, London, for
supplying equipment to be
photographed.

WARNING:

Water sports are highly enjoyable and good exercise, but water safety is the number one rule.

Beginners should learn the basics from a qualified instructor. Before signing up for diving instruction, check that you are old enough – the minimum age for diving varies from one country to another.

Even strong swimmers can sometimes get into trouble, so never swim in open water when there is any doubt about weather, tides or currents.

Don't swim alone, a rule also followed by sub-aqua divers, who always use the so-called 'buddy' system of swimming in pairs. Each diver looks after the other.

Kingfisher Books, Grisewood & Dempsey Ltd,
Elsley House, 24–30 Great Titchfield Street,
London W1P 7AD.

First published in 1990 by Kingfisher Books

BRITISH LIBRARY CATALOGUING IN PUBLICATION DATA
Jay, Michael
    Swimming and sub aqua.
    1. Swimming & diving. – For children
    I. Series
    797.2
    ISBN 0 86272 413 9

Phototypeset by Southern Positives and Negatives (SPAN),
Lingfield, Surrey
Printed in Spain

Contents

World of water

■ More than two-thirds of the surface of our planet is covered by water, and beneath the waves lies a hidden and mysterious region which air-breathing humans need special skills and equipment to explore. Fortunately, any fit and reasonably strong swimmer can enter this world by learning to use an aqualung, and there are numerous schools and clubs offering expert tuition. Safety comes first in water, so whether you are learning to swim or to dive, make sure you are taught by a qualified instructor.

▶ Aqualung divers enter a fascinating world of strange animals, beautiful plants and sunken ships.

▼ American swimmer Matthew Biondi set a 100 metre world record in June 1986, covering the distance in 48.74 seconds. For most people though, endurance is more important than speed.

Breast stroke

■ This popular stroke can be used in a variety of ways – for racing, for leisurely swimming and for life-saving and survival in rough water. It has two major advantages in that it is less tiring than other strokes, and it can be done with the face either in or out of the water.

As with all swimming strokes, breast stroke should be learnt in stages. You can leave practising swimming with your face in the water until you are comfortable with the arm and leg movements. The main difficulty at first is getting the correct rhythm. The steps below will help you to identify the various stages involved.

Breast stroke

Side view

▲▼ Floating on the water, stretch your body out flat, with the shoulders level with the water surface. Your eyes should be looking straight ahead, either just above or just below the surface. Hands and feet are stretched out full length.

▲▼ Sweep your arms out, down and back, keeping your hands flat or slightly cupped to push back against the water. Your feet trail behind. Without raising your head out of the water, breathe out as your arms finish the stroke.

▲▼ Sweep your hands round, forwards and in until they almost meet, bringing your elbows to your chest. Your legs are starting to bend. Push your chin forwards so your mouth pops out of the water long enough to take a breath.

Front view

∗ **The breast stroke swimming rhythm is: pull–breathe–kick–glide**

▲▼ Begin stretching your arms forwards again, just below the surface. At the same time, bend your legs up towards your bottom. Knees should point down and feet should stay hip-width apart, with the soles facing upwards.

▲▼ Continue the kick, with your legs moving together as they straighten. By now your toes should be pointing straight back once again, while your arms are stretched forwards ready for the next pull-stroke.

▲▼ While you are still reaching forwards, turn your feet out and kick your heels sharply backwards and slightly outwards. This 'whip kick' is faster and more powerful than the frog-like wedge kick often learnt by beginners.

Crawl

■ The front crawl is the fastest and the most efficient swimming stroke. It is nearly always chosen by competitors in freestyle races, and is also used for long-distance swimming.

Although front crawl is the easiest stroke to learn, it will take a while before you are used to putting your face in the water, and the breathing technique can cause difficulties at first. Start by making sure your body position is right, then add the leg kick, the arm action and the breathing.

Front crawl

▲ Lie flat, with your face in the water and your eyes looking forwards and down. Let your head be supported by the water. Kick up and down, one leg after the other – moving from the hips, *not* the knees.

▲ The arms should also work alternately. While one arm is pulling down and back, the other is lifting up and forwards, elbow high out of the water. Keep your fingers closed, like paddles.

▲ As the arm in the water completes its pull, start to turn your head and breathe out. The other hand is reaching forwards to enter the water between the shoulders and the body's centre line.

▲ As your elbow rises out of the water, finish turning your head. Lifting your arm over and forwards creates a trough in the water which should be deep enough to let you take a breath.

▲ This picture shows the right arm raised ready to go forwards, head turned to breathe, and the left arm just starting its power pull. After breathing in, return your head to the front.

▲ The right arm stretches forwards, while the left arm continues its pull. Try breathing on both sides, one breath every third arm pull. This way you can see what's going on around you.

Front crawl tips

☑ **Kicking from the hips will keep your body level. Deep-kicking is out because it lifts the head too high, while knee-kicking buries your head down in the water.**

☑ **Keep your fingers together. Having them apart is like paddling a canoe with a sieve.**

☑ **Swivel your head to breathe – don't lift it out of the water.**

☒ **Don't let your arms get too close to the centre line of your body, as this will make you roll from side to side.**

Practice tips

☑ **Beginners often find themselves red in the face from holding their breath when learning a new stroke. Try to relax and breathe regularly.**

☑ **Hold on to the side of the pool to practise your front-crawl breathing rhythm.**

☑ **Don't overtire yourself by making swimming sessions too long. For most people, and especially beginners, 30 minutes at a time is plenty. Vary strokes, too – try a different one every 10 minutes or so.**

Back crawl

Try this stroke for a change or if you can't master breathing during the front crawl. The back crawl is a good stroke for anyone who doesn't like putting their face under water. You can't see where you are going, but you can roll over every now and then to check the coast is clear. You can use either a bent arm pull as shown here or a straight-arm action, sweeping them out to the sides.

▲ **With arm and hand out straight, the arm enters the water in line with the shoulder, upper arm brushing your ear. Your feet maintain a steady up-down rhythm.**

▲ **Pull your hand down alongside your body and towards your feet. As you pull, your elbow bends and the palm of your hand swivels round to face the feet.**

▲ **The pull stroke ends as the elbow straightens. Flick your hand out and down as your other arm straightens ahead, with the palm facing out.**

▲ **The right arm starts its power pull while the left arm lifts clear of the water. Keep a steady arm-and-leg rhythm, feet hardly breaking the water surface.**

▲ **The right arm continues its power pull, while the left arm nearly brushes your ear. Try and avoid splashing, as this simply wastes energy.**

Butterfly dolphin

■ This stroke needs a lot of strength. Until you have developed good endurance with breast stroke and crawl, it's unlikely that you will manage more than a few butterfly strokes at a time.

A key point to remember is to keep the legs and feet together, moving them up and down continuously. Breathing is easier than for the crawl, as the butterfly action naturally brings the head up and out of the water.

▶ The great American butterfly swimmer Mary Meagher. In August 1981 she set a world record for the 100 metres of 57.93 seconds.

Butterfly dolphin

▲ The arms and legs work together. Here the arms are arched forwards, with palms cupped downwards, just about to enter the water. The legs are beginning to thrust down.

▲ As the arms pull down and out through the water, the legs should straighten to end the downward thrust. The head is now at its lowest point in the stroke.

▲ The arms continue pulling down and back, while the legs pump upwards to complete their first down-and-up movement. Keep your body as level as you can throughout the stroke.

▲ As your arms pass your shoulder line, start to push against the water. Push back strongly to complete the stroke. Your legs begin their second downward thrust.

▲ The arms leave the water elbows first. This arches the back up, raising the head to its highest point in the stroke – it's time to take a deep breath.

▲ As the arms swing out and forwards past the shoulders, the head goes back into the water. Meanwhile, the legs are completing their second down-and-up movement.

Taking the plunge

■ Diving lessons can begin when you are happy jumping into the deep end and swimming underwater with your eyes open. Below are the stages you can progress through. The plunge dive makes a flying start to a swimming race. Stretch out and try for a shallow entry into the water. Glide, then raise your head to surface.

▶ This diver displays a perfect vertical body position as he plunges into the water, the clean entry making only a small splash.

▲ Sit with your feet on the swimming pool trough. Raise your arms, tuck in your head, and bend over until you tip forwards into the water.

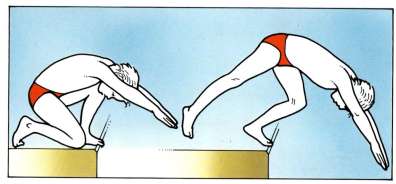

▲ Kneeling on one knee, grip the edge of the trough with the toes of your front foot. Raise your arms and tuck in your head, as for the sitting dive. Then lean over forwards until you overbalance and tip into the water. Push off with your front foot and stretch forwards and down into the water.

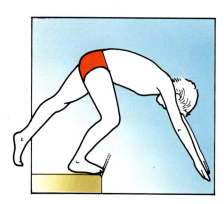

▲ To lunge dive, stand with one foot forward and knees slightly bent, gripping the edge with your front toes. Try to bring your legs together as you tip in.

▲ Crouch with your toes curled round the edge. Raise your arms and tuck in your head. As you tip in, try to straighten your legs to get a steep entry into the water.

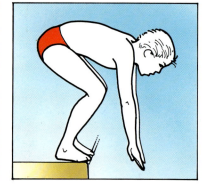

▲ To plunge dive, crouch on the side, arms down, head up, looking at where you want to hit the water. Swing your arms up, tip forwards and thrust off, out and down.

Water safety

☑ **Watch out for other people, and never practise diving if there are a lot of people in the pool. You could hurt someone by landing on top of them.**
☑ **Look out for the bottom of the pool as well – it's easy to run out of room and graze your hands or hit your head.**
☑ **Don't dive into water which is too shallow. The** *minimum* **safe depth for a vertical dive from poolside level is your height plus your stretched-up arms. It's more from a board.**

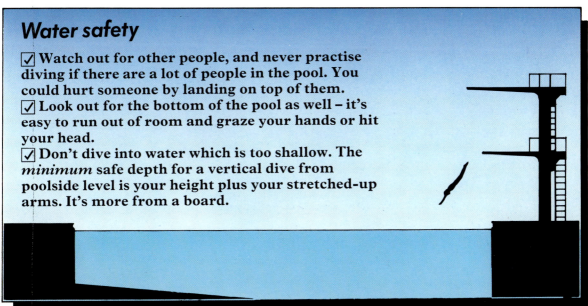

Headers and pikes

■ Learning how to dive will add to your confidence in the water, and as with the basic swimming strokes the trick is to take your time and master each step along the way. Work level by level – don't try high dives until you can dive well from the poolside.

▶ American Greg Louganis has won many world diving titles. Here he holds his body in a piked position before straightening up to hit the water.

Plain header dive

This dive is often used by competitors in diving events, from either the side of the pool or a board. Bend your knees, keeping your weight on the balls of your feet. Spring hard, keeping your arms straight. Arc over the water then straighten into the plunge, aiming as always for a smooth entry.

▶ Although they have many variations, there are three basic diving positions for the body:
1. Completely straight.
2. Piked – body bent sharply at the hips, legs straight.
3. Tucked – body curled into a ball shape, bent knees held by the hands.

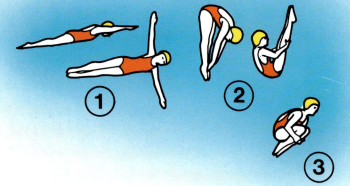

Voyage to inner space

■ For thousands of years the only way to explore underwater was to hold your breath as you went under the surface. In 1690, English scientist Edmund Halley devised his diving bell, a large air-filled barrel from which divers could work at a depth of over 16 metres. Sealed buckets of air could be sent down to refresh the bell's limited breathing supply. Twenty-five years later John Lethbridge produced a diving machine in which he made many dives. Another major step forward came in 1819, when German engineer Augustus Siebe produced a metal helmet diving suit. Later improvements made suits based on Siebe's designs standard equipment until the invention of lightweight aqualung gear in the 1940s.

▲ Englishman John Lethbridge built this wooden diving machine in 1715. His lifeline was a tube down which fresh air was pumped by bellows, from a boat on the surface. Although Lethbridge could dive no deeper than 20 metres, he successfully recovered valuables from a number of wrecked ships lying on the sea bed.

▲ Siebe's diving suit of 1819 had a metal helmet with thick glass windows in the front and sides. Air was pumped into the helmet through a tube from the surface.

The aqualung

In 1942 Frenchmen Emile Gagnon and Jacques Cousteau perfected a new type of breathing equipment for divers. They named it the aqualung, and its most important feature was a demand valve that regulated the air a diver breathed. Earlier valves had given continuous air flow, which allowed most of it to bubble away to waste. The new demand valve corrected this, giving the exact amount of air needed at any time during a dive.

▼ Another word for aqualung is scuba, which stands for self-contained underwater breathing apparatus. Scuba divers always explore in groups of two. This 'buddy' system is for safety reasons – it ensures that there is always someone to help if a diver gets into trouble.

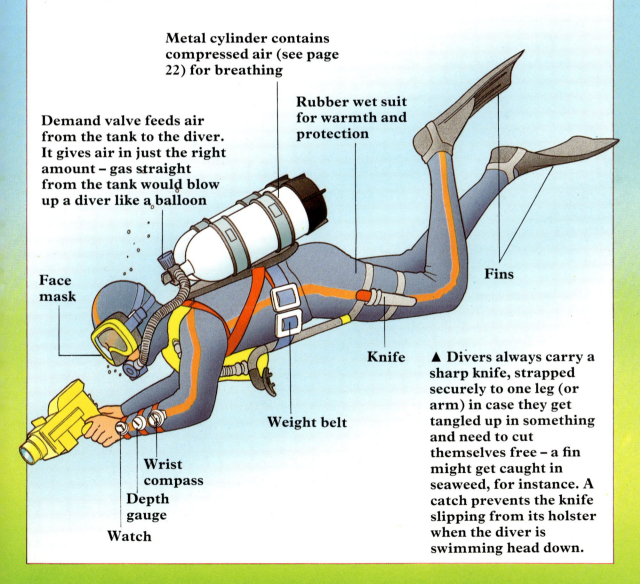

Metal cylinder contains compressed air (see page 22) for breathing

Rubber wet suit for warmth and protection

Demand valve feeds air from the tank to the diver. It gives air in just the right amount – gas straight from the tank would blow up a diver like a balloon

Face mask

Fins

Knife

Weight belt

Wrist compass

Depth gauge

Watch

▲ Divers always carry a sharp knife, strapped securely to one leg (or arm) in case they get tangled up in something and need to cut themselves free – a fin might get caught in seaweed, for instance. A catch prevents the knife slipping from its holster when the diver is swimming head down.

Mask, snorkel and fins

■ Learning how to use a mask and snorkel is an important part of learning to dive. Snorkeling is a fascinating sport in its own right, especially in warm clear water full of colourful marine life. And with a pair of fins on your feet, you'll be able to glide along as easily as one of the fish you'll be watching.

▼ The snorkel tube lets you breathe through your mouth while gliding along on or just below the water surface. The mouthpiece fits between lips and gums, and is held gently with the teeth. The snorkel is held at the correct angle by fastening it to the mask strap. If water sloshes in, clear the tube by blowing out like a whale.

▼ There are many different fin designs, though they all do the same job, improving the propelling efficiency of your feet. Using fins, you can move through the water with little effort. Some fins have adjustable straps; others have slip-on fittings.

Fin with adjustable footstrap

Plastic or rubber snorkel tube

Mouthpiece with toothgrips

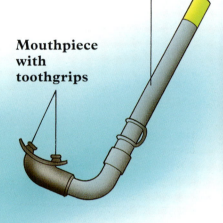

Adjustable strap

General purpose fin with slip-on foot section

◄ Masks come in as many shapes as fins. Smaller ones are often best as glass near your eyes makes for wider vision underwater. Check for comfort and fit – a loose mask will let in water. To stop a mask misting up, rub spit on the inner glass, then rinse it out with seawater and put it on.

Finning

With fins on, lie on your back at the shallow end of a swimming pool. Beat your legs up and down in a crawl stroke – the fins push against the water to propel you along. Try not to break the surface with the fins or you lose thrust. As you move ahead, roll over onto your front, raising your head to breathe. Once you feel happy with the fins, try the same exercise wearing mask and snorkel.

Duck diving

Try this at the deep end of the pool once you have got the hang of snorkeling on the surface. Floating full length, take a deep breath and bend down from the waist. When you are pointing to the bottom of the pool, flip your fins up and slide down, moving the fins as soon as they go under the water. Level out at the bottom of the pool, swim along for a few seconds then return to the surface. Blow any water out of the snorkel when you get there.

Dressed to dive

■ In tropical climates, divers need no special clothing as the waters are warm, at least in the top layers of the sea where divers mostly swim. In cooler parts of the world, suits like those shown below are essential. Rubber boots and gloves can be worn to keep hands and feet warm.

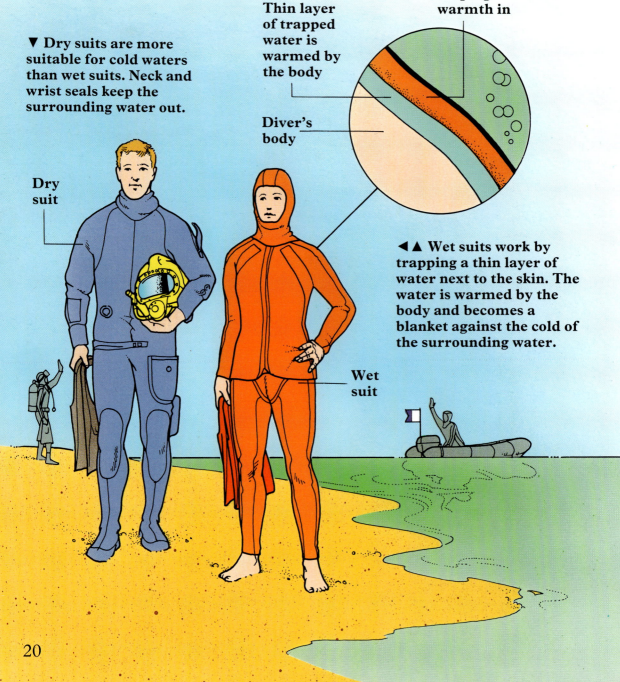

Rubber wet suit acts as an insulator, keeping warmth in

Thin layer of trapped water is warmed by the body

Diver's body

▼ Dry suits are more suitable for cold waters than wet suits. Neck and wrist seals keep the surrounding water out.

Dry suit

◄▲ Wet suits work by trapping a thin layer of water next to the skin. The water is warmed by the body and becomes a blanket against the cold of the surrounding water.

Wet suit

▲ A lifejacket is normally worn on every dive. This lifejacket can be inflated with air from the backpack cylinder to bring a diver to the surface or to adjust buoyancy to float at a particular depth. Other equipment includes a weight belt, necessary to allow a diver to sink easily.

▶ A wrist compass is worn to keep a direction check. A watch is used to keep a check on the dive time. Many watches have an alarm to warn when the dive time is up.

Underwater air supply

■ Scuba divers can swim about freely underwater because they carry their air with them. So that more of it can be carried, the air is compressed, or squashed, into a metal cylinder which is strapped to a backpack. The air is also filtered, to remove moisture and impurities which could prove dangerous if breathed in during a dive. Once underwater, the pressure and amount of the diver's air are regulated by the demand valve.

▼ Here, used air is bubbling away from a diver's mouthpiece. As a diver descends further below the surface the pressure of the water on the body greatly increases. Without the demand-valve system, which supplies air at a matching pressure, the diver's lungs would be crushed.

▶ Most aqualungs have these components:
1. Demand valve
2. Tap for turning air supply on and off
3. Compressed-air cylinder
4. Clamp to attach cylinder to backpack
5. Backpack to take weight of cylinder
6. Mouthpiece
7. Air line to lifejacket
8. Shoulder straps
9. Pressure gauge to measure air in cylinder
10. Waist strap with quick-release buckle

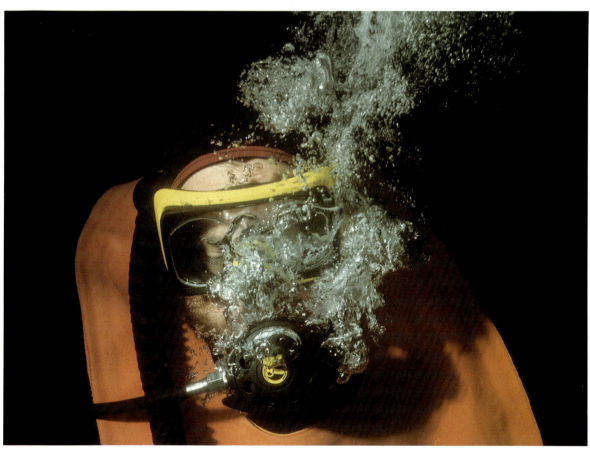

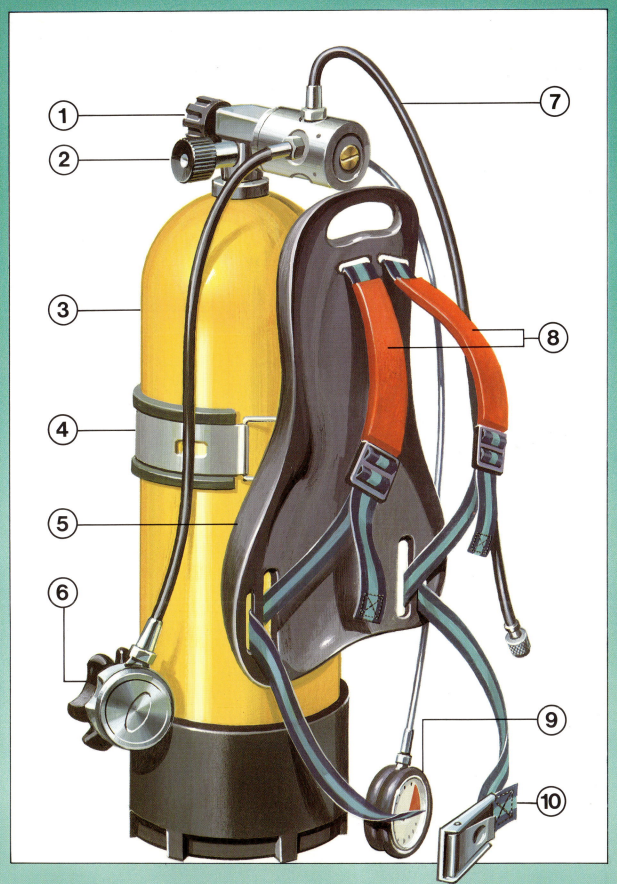

First dives

■ It's usual for divers to do all their basic training, including using an aqualung, in a swimming pool. Only when a diver is comfortable with the equipment, and familiar with diving safety and rules, is it time to take to open water. You'll be paired with a buddy before each dive, and you'll be briefed on where and how deep you're going, and how long the dive is scheduled to last.

▶ Divers push their inflatable boat into the surf. When diving from an inflatable, it's normal to sit on the side and roll over backwards. Hold your mask firmly to your face.

▼ Before the dive, your instructor outlines the dive plan, briefing you on what's to come. You check your equipment – have you got everything? Is it working?

▼ Walk backwards into the water – try going forwards and you'll trip over your fins. Turn round when you are waist deep. At chest level, fit your mask and mouthpiece.

▼ Lean forwards next and breathe out to check whether you are heavy enough to sink. If you are too light, return to land and add more weight to your belt.

▼ Holding on to the line from the buoy (see page 29), sink slowly, feet first. Clear your ears gently as you go down. Do everything carefully, making sure you get it right.

▼ Using hand signals, your instructor checks that you are all right and points out the direction to go. With a flick of your fins, you set off swimming alongside.

▼ Following your instructor closely, you see a dim shape ahead. The water slowly clears to reveal a seaweed-covered ship. You're about to explore your first wreck!

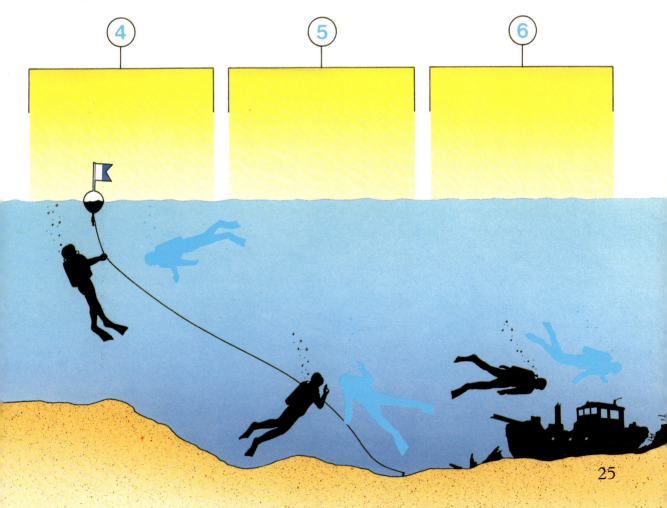

Checks and dangers

■ Sub-aqua, like other adventure sports, is not as simple as catching a bus, and various hazards are involved. But expert tuition and careful planning make it a sport that the vast majority of divers enjoy in safety. Among the basic rules is to have a medical check before you start diving, to make sure you are fit to go underwater.

Personal fitness

☑ **No diving unless passed as fit by doctor, with a chest X-ray to check the lungs are in good order. Adults have medical checks at regular intervals to ensure they are in good physical shape for continued diving.**
☑ **There should be no diving when under the influence of drugs or alcohol – even taking seasickness pills can make a diver drowsy.**
☑ **No sub-aqua if you have a cold or flu. Diving with blocked passages can damage ear drums.**

Equipment checks

☑ **Ensure that your equipment is in good working order.**
☑ **Check very carefully for small nicks or cuts in air hoses.**
☑ **Lines should all be clipped on neatly. Check that none of your equipment is caught or snagged.**
☑ **Make sure your air tank is filled with air at the correct pressure.**

Buddy check

Buddies are responsible for each other's safety underwater, so a pre-dive buddy check is carried out, noting that all the other diver's equipment is in place, connected and working properly.

Tank test

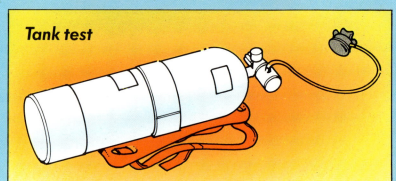

A faulty air tank could leak or, at worst, explode like a bomb, so tanks are inspected regularly. A test stamp is engraved into the thickest part of the tank, up on its shoulder. Before a dive, hoses and valves are checked for condition and leaks.

During a dive

Visibility can often be just a few metres or less. In murky water, buddies can rope together to avoid loss of contact. Divers must take care not to get too cold, easily done when swimming in chilly northern waters. Loss of 'core' temperature in the body – hypothermia – can be a killer.

The narcs

The bends (see below) are not the only hazard posed by breathing in nitrogen. On deep dives, there is also the risk of nitrogen narcosis, or 'the narcs'. This produces effects similar to those of alcohol – loss of concentration, confusion and drowsiness. Fortunately, there are no harmful after-effects.

The bends (decompression sickness)

Normally, the nitrogen gas we breathe in from the air causes us no problems. But on a deep dive, the pressure of the water helps it to pass very easily into the bloodstream. If a diver comes up too quickly, nitrogen bubbles form in the body – like the gas in an opened bottle of fizzy drink. This leads to 'the bends', so called because divers bend and twist their bodies to relieve the agony.

At best, the bends cause only mild aches ('the niggles'), but in extreme circumstances they can kill. To avoid this unpleasant problem, divers need to come up slowly and in stages, following the guidelines set out in charts known as decompression tables.

Back to the boat

On the way to the surface, divers stick to the correct ascent times to avoid any danger of the bends. Back on the boat, lightweight windproof jackets are worn as protection from the wind as it's easy to catch a chill when you are exposed to the elements.

Talking underwater

■ Divers communicate with each other by using a simple hand-signal system. This is an international code, so the signals should mean the same wherever you dive. Even so, divers always check, before going under, what signals are being used, to avoid possible confusion later on. A popular way to attract attention is to knock your air tank with the handle of your knife – the clang carries some way through the water.

▲ 'Stop'. Like the raised hand of a policeman.

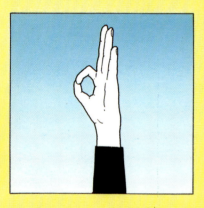

▲ 'OK, all is well'. Can be a question or the same signal returned to confirm that you are OK.

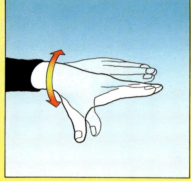

▲ 'Something wrong'. A hand rocked from side to side indicates a problem needing attention.

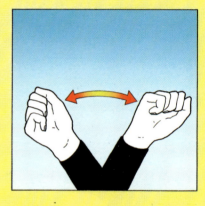

▲ 'Distress'. Waving a clenched fist from side to side shows the diver needs immediate help.

▲ 'Go up', 'I am going up'. Clenched fist with upraised thumb, one of the direction signals.

▲ 'Go down', 'I am going down'. Clenched fist signal, usually used only at the start of a dive.

▲ 'You or me'. Diver points to the diver who will be referred to in the signal that follows.

▲ 'I am out of breath'. Moving hands in and out from your lungs shows that you need a rest.

▲ 'I am on reserve'. Shows that the air supply is low and it's time to return to the surface.

▲ 'I have no air'. Seeing this signal, buddies will come close to share air with dive partners.

Surface marker buoys

Surface marker buoys, called SMBs for short, are used to identify the position of divers during a dive. SMBs are essential when tides or currents could sweep divers a long way from their cover boat on the surface. The dive leader carries a reel of line attached to a brightly coloured float with a flag on top.

SMB

Cover boat

Line

Dive leader

Exploring the seas

■ One of the great excitements of scuba diving is the chance to search sunken wrecks for hidden treasure. Fortunes are rarely made, but the lure of a forgotten cargo of gold bullion or a safe full of diamonds is a strong one. There's a different kind of wealth to be gained from discovering how people lived in the past though, and there are probably more archaeologists underwater than treasure seekers!

▼ **A diver looks out from inside the rusting hulk of an old cargo ship. Plants grow on the vessel's structure and inside its gloomy hold.**

Diving around the world

These are some of the world's best spots for diving on wrecks and for viewing the more colourful species of marine life. The icy waters towards the north and south poles are out of the question for most divers, since defeating the cold requires special equipment. Nearer to the equator, the warmer water is far more pleasant for diving.

Pacific Ocean
Warm tropical waters and colourful marine life make the Pacific islands popular with divers. World War II wrecks can be seen off some islands.

British Isles
There are probably more sunken wrecks off the coast of Britain than anywhere else in the world. Sea life includes seals and basking sharks.

Red Sea
Famous for its crystal-clear warm waters, the strange shapes of its coral reefs, and the brilliant colours of the underwater creatures that live there.

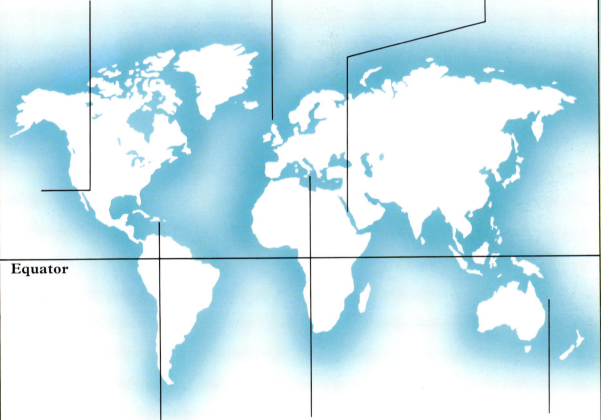

Equator

Caribbean Sea
Much of the water around the Caribbean islands is shallow, clear and warm, making the region highly suitable for beginners. Marine life includes the odd-looking but harmless dugong, or sea cow.

Mediterranean Sea
Many wrecks dating back 2000 or more years, to Roman and Ancient Greek times, have been found in these waters, but removal of objects such as pottery jugs is illegal without a special licence.

Great Barrier Reef
At over 2000 km long, this area off Australia's north-eastern coast is the longest coral reef in the world. Its stunning marine life can be seen through glass-bottomed boats, as well as by diving.

The living oceans

■ The oceans are teeming with life, from surface to sea bed. Marine creatures come in endless shapes, sizes, colours and patterns. Bottom-dwelling fish tend to be sandy-hued to blend in with the ocean floor while fish that live in reefs are often brightly coloured to match the shades of the corals.

Scuba divers are usually wise to look but not touch – few plants or animals are killers, but many can inflict nasty wounds on unprotected human flesh!

► An underwater world of colour and beauty awaits divers off the shores of the Red Sea, a paradise area for underwater explorers.

▼ Here are some of the sea creatures a diver shouldn't touch – they all sting, bite or have poison barbs.

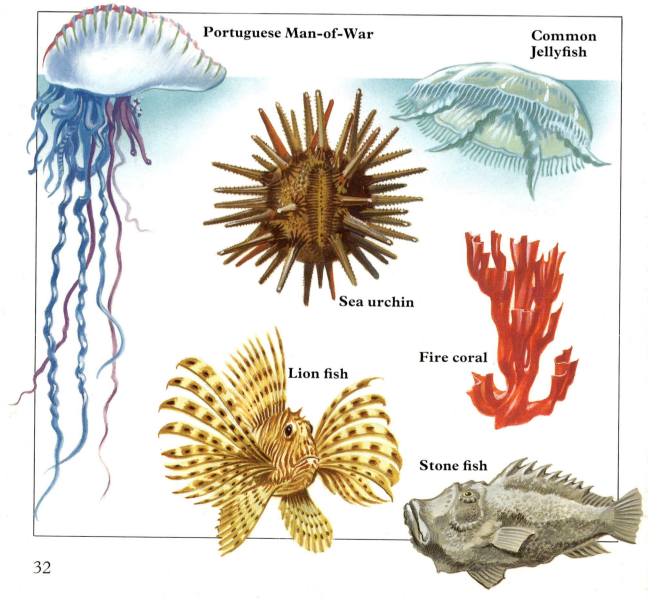

Portuguese Man-of-War

Common Jellyfish

Sea urchin

Fire coral

Lion fish

Stone fish

Shark!

■ Sharks are among the most feared creatures in the oceans, although attacks on humans are fairly rare. Despite their reputation, few sharks are really dangerous – of the 250 or so species, fewer than 30 are confirmed man-eaters. In fact, the biggest species, the 16-metre-long whale shark, feeds on tiny shrimp-like plankton, gulping them from the sea as it thrusts its vast bulk through the water. Even so, sharks are unpredictable creatures and divers treat them with caution.

▼ This strange sight is a baby hammerhead shark. At the moment it is no menace, but a fully-grown hammerhead is one of the most dangerous sharks of all. It grows to a length of four metres or more.

Sharks big and small

The shark family ranges from the huge whale shark to smaller species such as the dogfish, which grows less than a metre long. In between there are sharks of all sizes. Sharks mostly hunt alone, but the smell and taste of blood is enough to bring them together as a pack, gathered in a 'feeding frenzy' when they will attack anything, including each other.

The sharks shown here are all dangerous. They live in and around the reefs of tropical and sub-tropical waters.

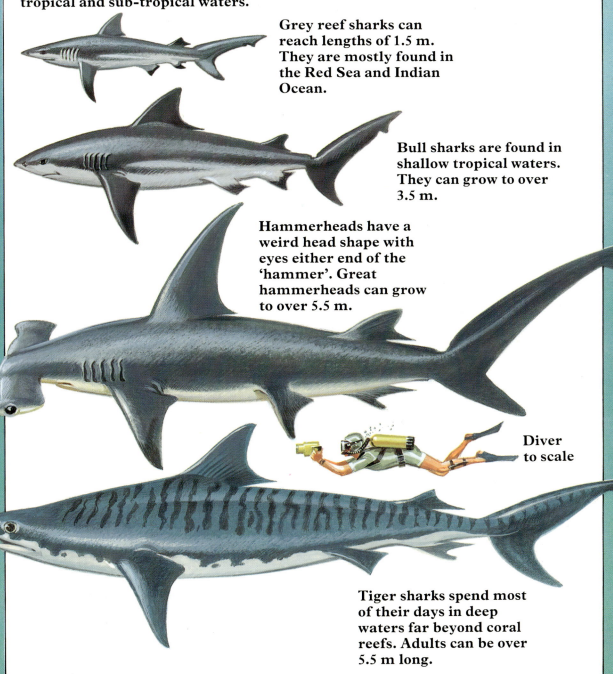

Grey reef sharks can reach lengths of 1.5 m. They are mostly found in the Red Sea and Indian Ocean.

Bull sharks are found in shallow tropical waters. They can grow to over 3.5 m.

Hammerheads have a weird head shape with eyes either end of the 'hammer'. Great hammerheads can grow to over 5.5 m.

Diver to scale

Tiger sharks spend most of their days in deep waters far beyond coral reefs. Adults can be over 5.5 m long.

Photographs and videos

■ There's a fairly wide range of still and video cameras suitable for underwater use. The cheaper ones can only be used in the shallows – cameras sealed against the higher water pressures at depth are very expensive. But since most marine life is found near the surface, even simple equipment.will give you colourful dive records.

Light unit

Big, easy-to-use control knobs

Flash unit

Waterproof housings

▲ This is typical of the waterproof 35-mm cameras you'll find in a good photographic equipment shop. It is suitable only for shallow water.

The camera body is made of toughened plastic, with oversized controls that are easy to use even when you're wearing diving gloves. The built-in flash and film wind-on are both automatic.

▶ For great action shots, take a special underwater video camera down with you. The camera controls are worked by using extensions mounted on the outside of the housing. The model shown here includes a powerful light unit mounted on the top and an underwater microphone – imagine recording the moaning cry of a whale!

Of the various video systems on the market, Video-8 is probably the most suitable for sub-aqua work as the tapes last up to 90 minutes, enough for a feature-length underwater epic. There's no chance to reload in mid-dive!

◄ Close encounter with a grey seal, a marine mammal which can reach a length of 2.3 m. Seals belong to an animal order called the pinnipeds – amphibious mammals with paddle-like limbs – which also includes sea lions and walruses. This photograph was taken off the coast of Britain.

▼ Many plants and animals make their homes in sunken wrecks. Here a spider crab clings onto an old ship's girder.

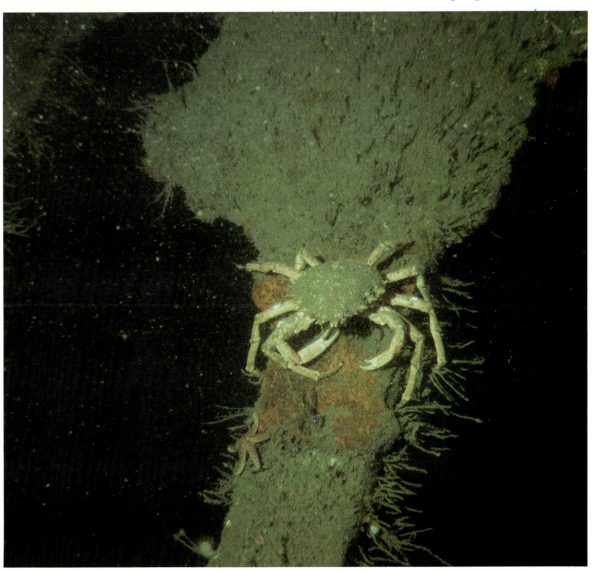

Glossary

Buddy
Safety practice of diving in pairs, so that divers can look after each other and be on hand in case of emergencies. For example, if a diver has problems with his air supply, he can use his buddy's air, the two divers sharing the same mouthpiece.

Compressed air
High-pressure air pumped into a scuba tank. The air is filtered to remove impurities before it enters the tank. The demand-valve system ensures a diver gets only the correct amount of air needed for each breath. As depth increases, so does water pressure, so the demand valve supplies air at a matching pressure, to avoid the diver's lungs being crushed by the surrounding water.

Decompression time
Length of time taken to return to the surface, making allowance for nitrogen to pass out of the body, so avoiding the bends. Decompression tables show the times required to come up from various depths. Divers ascend in stages, pausing for a time at various levels up to the surface.

Demand valve
Mechanical system designed to provide a diver with air from the backpack air cylinder. Supplies air 'on demand', hence the name.

Dive plan
Aqualung dives begin with a pre-dive briefing, given by the dive marshal, the person in charge of the diving group. The marshal explains the purpose of the dive, what each diver is to do, equipment checks, any particular problems and any special signals for the mission. Divers are teamed up as buddies, with one as leader. When the dive is over the dive marshal gives a de-briefing, in which questions or problems can be discussed.

Dry suit
Sealed diving suit, designed to keep the wearer dry. The warmth of such a suit means a diver can spend several hours in the water without getting chilled. There are two types of dry suit – neoprene (the synthetic rubber material used for wet suits) and membrane. The membrane suit is made of thinner material and to keep warm, divers need to wear nylon-fur undergarments nicknamed 'woolly bears'.

In addition to keeping divers warm, both dry and wet suits give a degree of protection from cuts, grazes and stings.

Freestyle
Competition event in which swimmers can select whichever stroke they wish.

Hypothermia
Loss of temperature in the central core area of the body. In temperatures of less than about 21°C, water conducts heat away faster than the body can replace it. So in a short time, any unclothed person will become chilled. Wet suits provide good protection in temperatures down to about 10°C. In colder waters, dry suits should be worn.

Lifejacket
Several types are made, but the all-round one is the ABLJ adjustable buoyancy life jacket. The best ABLJs have three methods of inflation – by mouth, by a mini-cylinder on the jacket or by a direct feed hose from the backpack cylinder. ABLJs can be used to adjust a diver's buoyancy during a dive,

▲ Metal helmet diving gear, developed from Augustus Siebe's first suit, was widely used until the invention of scuba equipment. 'Hard hat' suits like this are still in use today. Heavily weighted boots and a metal helmet with portholes are features of this type of equipment.

enabling the diver to 'hover' at different depths. In an emergency an ABLJ can bring a diver to the surface. Once on the surface it keeps the diver's head above the water.

Piked
Mid-air diving position, legs straight, body sharply bent at the waist.

Scuba
Self-contained underwater breathing apparatus. Another name for the aqualung equipment developed by Jacques Cousteau and Emile Gagnon. Cousteau become famous for his underwater research work.

Surface marker buoy
Flag mounted on a bright coloured float, to show position of divers under the water. Especially useful when divers are swimming in currents, when they will drift from the position in which they started the dive.

Tucked
Position held briefly in mid-air during a dive, with the body curled into a ball, legs held with the arms.

Weight belt
The buoyancy of the human body and protective clothing means that lead weights must be added to enable a diver to achieve neutral buoyancy – floating underwater, neither rising nor falling. The amount of weight needed varies from diver to diver, but a typical medium-build adult might have 6 kg wearing a wet suit, or 10 kg wearing a dry suit.

Wet suit
Lightweight rubber protective suit which works by trapping a thin layer of water between the suit and the body.

Index